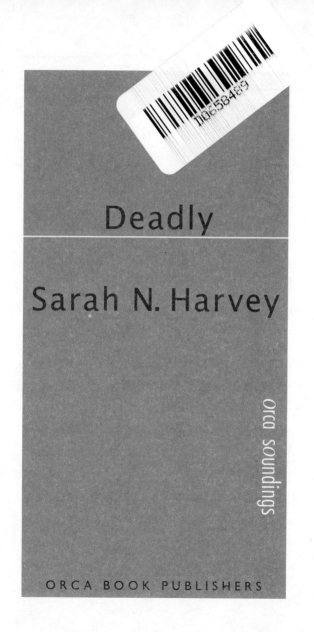

Deadly

Sarah N. Harvey

orca soundings

ORCA BOOK PUBLISHERS

Library and Archives Canada Cataloguing in Publication

Harvey, Sarah N., 1950-
Deadly / Sarah Harvey.
(Orca soundings)

Issued also in electronic formats.
ISBN 978-1-4598-0365-7 (bound).--ISBN 978-1-4598-0364-0 (pbk.)

I. Title. II. Series: Orca soundings
PS8615.A764D41 2013   jc813'.6   C2012-907483-7

First published in the United States, 2013
Library of Congress Control Number: 2012952956

Summary: Amy may be a sinner, but she's not a coward.

MIX
Paper from
responsible sources
FSC® C016245
www.fsc.org

*Orca Book Publishers is dedicated to preserving the environment and has printed
this book on Forest Stewardship Council® certified paper.*

Orca Book Publishers gratefully acknowledges the support for its publishing
programs provided by the following agencies: the Government of Canada through
the Canada Book Fund and the Canada Council for the Arts,
and the Province of British Columbia through the BC Arts Council
and the Book Publishing Tax Credit.

Cover photography by Getty Images

ORCA BOOK PUBLISHERS
PO Box 5626, Stn. B
Victoria, BC Canada
V8R 6S4

ORCA BOOK PUBLISHERS
PO Box 468
Custer, WA USA
98240-0468

www.orcabook.com
Printed and bound in Canada.

16 15 14 13 • 4 3 2 1

Chapter One

Amy

I wake up in a white room. Not my room, which is the color of a robin's egg. Not Eric's room, which is navy blue (his mom said no to black) and smells like teenage boy. You know—sweat and junk food and unwashed sheets and other nasty stuff. I don't go there a lot. Eric says he likes my house better anyway. My mom often works late, the sheets are clean, there's always food in the fridge, and my older sister, Beth, is cool. My name is Amy. Our mother named us after the two youngest sisters in *Little Women*. To say my mother is a bookworm is an understatement. At least I wasn't named after the sister who dies.

I squint around the white room and wonder if I am in a hospital. But it's too quiet. I've been in the ER enough times in my sixteen years to know that it sounds like pain and smells like fear. All I hear in the white room is a faint hum. And the room smells like… nothing. No leftover cooking smells, no stale perfume, no wilting flowers. Nothing. I duck my head under the white duvet and inhale deeply. Familiar smells—cucumber body wash, lavender shampoo, a whiff of Mom's rose-scented lotion. She's a hugger. I think I can detect a hint of Eric's deodorant.

He's a hugger too. I smile under the covers. Mom and Eric, both rubbing off on me. In totally different ways.

Why am I smiling? I don't know where I am, and I have a massive headache. I can't be hung over. I don't drink that much. Not anymore. Not since Beth's accident.

The bed I am lying in is very comfortable. If I wasn't starting to feel kind of freaked out, I'd roll over and go back to sleep in my white cocoon. I'm so tired. I stick my head out from under the covers and look around again, trying to focus, but everything is a bit blurry. When I try to sit up, a wave of nausea knocks me down. I stare at the ceiling for a while. Maybe for a minute. Maybe for an hour. It's hard to tell. My mouth is so dry. I turn my head and notice a bottle of water on a small table beside the bed. Very slowly, I reach out for it and prop myself up enough to drink. It takes all my strength to open the bottle. The first sip is so delicious. I tip the bottle back and chug as much as I can, as fast as I can. A lot of it goes down my chin and neck and onto my chest. I don't care. Nothing has ever tasted this good. For a minute anyway.

The nausea roars back, and I know I'm going to puke. I stand up and am almost flattened by a tsunami of dizziness. I steady myself against the white wall and feel my way along it until I reach a doorway. A doorway to what turns out to be a small white bathroom. I stagger over to the toilet and retch violently. When I am done, I pull some white towels off a rack, make a nest on the floor and pass out again.

When I wake up, the nausea has passed, but my whole body aches. Every muscle.

Every joint. Every bone. Even my hair hurts. And my toenails. I groan and drag myself up to lean against the wall. So far, so good. I wonder whose apartment I'm in. And how I got here. And what day it is. And why I'm alone. I stand in the bathroom doorway and look around. The apartment is one big room—a studio. A small kitchen is tucked into one corner of the room. There's a mini-fridge but no stove. The small round kitchen table has one chair. Three square white wicker baskets are lined up against the wall opposite the bed. Everything is white. And there are no windows. This freaks me out more than anything. Who builds an apartment with no windows? Who lives in one? And where is the light coming from? The room isn't dark, and the pot lights aren't on. I look up and realize that there is a double row of glass blocks where two of the walls meet the ceiling.

Even if I could get up there, I wouldn't be able to see through the blocks.

From where I'm standing, I can see every inch of the place, but I call out, "Hello? Anybody here?" in case I've missed something—another door, a loft, a secret staircase. I am met with silence. I stagger over to the kitchen and open the fridge. It's jammed with Tetra Paks of milk and juice. There's a loaf of multigrain bread, a head of leafy lettuce, a few tomatoes, some carrots, a package of Kraft Singles, three apples and three oranges. My stomach lurches. Whoever has brought me here isn't planning on feeding me for long. I'm not sure if that's good or bad. Under the sink is a blue recycling bin, the only hit of color in the whole place.

One cupboard is full of paper plates, bowls and cups, all made from recycled material. Another cupboard reveals a selection of organic cereal.

Buckwheat. Kamut. Ugh. There's a jar of peanut butter too. The kind I hate, made with sugar. One drawer holds bamboo cutlery. Another holds small packets of sugar, salt, pepper, ketchup, mustard, mayo and soy sauce—the kind you get in fast-food restaurants. Weird. A third drawer is full of lined yellow notepads and Sharpies. Weirder.

I head back to the bathroom and find miniature bottles of shampoo and conditioner in the glass shower stall (there's no bathtub), some small bars of wrapped soap and a selection of sample-size body lotions and hand creams. The counter beside the sink holds Kleenex, a pink toothbrush (ooh—more color!) and a travel-size tube of tooth-paste. Under the sink is a stack of toilet paper. Am I in a hotel? It feels impersonal, like no one lives here.

I'm starting to feel dizzy again—and scared. I need to sit down. I make my way slowly to the table and collapse into the molded-plastic chair. On the table is something I hadn't noticed before: a white envelope. With my name on it.

Chapter Two

Eric

Amy isn't answering her phone or responding to texts. That's not like her at all. Even when we're fighting, she always wants to talk. We joke about the four words no guy ever wants to hear: We need to talk. With Amy, it's all about communication. She says it's because she watched her parents' marriage shrivel up and die. Like a plant getting no water, she says. And talking is the water on the plant of a relationship. She actually says shit like that. Her parents broke up after Beth's accident. So we talk. A lot. When we can't talk, we text. So this isn't like her. Not like her at all.

I call her house and Beth answers.

"Is Amy there?" I ask.

"Don't think so," Beth says. "Hang on. I'll check." I can hear her yelling Amy's name. Then she comes back on the line. "Nope, not here. And she was gonna drive me to physio. When you talk to her, tell her to call me."

"Okay," I say. After I hang up, I start calling Amy's friends—our friends. People who were at the party last night. No one has seen her, and almost everyone asks me why the hell I'm calling so early.

"It's eleven o'clock already," I say, over and over.

"Dude," Cole says, "she's probably at that chick Shawna's place. They were dancing last night. Girl on girl. It was hot. I thought you were gonna get some three-way action."

"Shut up," I say, even though I agree. It *was* hot, and I had thought about the possibilities. None of us really know Shawna. She doesn't go to our school, and I don't have her number. No idea where she lives. Or if she'd ever do a three-way.

My phone rings. Amy's home number.

"Where have you been?" I say when I pick up.

"Uh, Eric. It's me, Beth. Mom just got up. She's asking where Amy is. Any luck with your friends?"

"Eric? Eric?" Amy's mom comes on the line. Another kind of three-way. Gross. How can I even be thinking about stuff like that when Amy is missing?

Missing. She can't be. She's probably at Shawna's house, wherever that is.

"Hi, Ms. Lessard. I haven't seen Amy since last night. At the party."

"What party?"

Oh shit. Amy told her mom she was going to Monica's place to work on a dance routine. Ms. Lessard is very down on parties. It occurs to me that *down on* is the opposite of *down with*. I smile to myself. Amy would think that was funny too.

"Eric? What party? Where?"

When I don't answer right away she says, "Eric, I don't care about the party. I just need to know where she is."

"I left the party early—we had a fight."

"A fight?"

"Yeah. No big deal. I wanted to go, she wanted to stay. She said she'd call a cab to get home."

"You left her there. Alone." It sounds more like a statement than an accusation. But I still feel the need to defend myself. Ms. Lessard is always nice to me, but I don't think she trusts me, exactly.

"Her friends were there. And she wasn't drunk or anything. And she'd never get a ride with someone who'd been drinking. Never. You know that."

There's silence on the other end of the line, as if both Beth and her mother are holding their breath. Remembering.

"Call me if you hear anything, Eric," Ms. Lessard finally says. "Anything at all."

I ride my bike over to the party house—or what I think is the party house. It's in a neighborhood I don't usually go to. The houses are old and run-down and chopped into apartments.

The front yards are mostly paved over and filled with crap—rusty car parts, battered kids' toys. Lots of chain-link fencing and bars over windows. But there's the house. I know it's the right one because I remember the neon Bud Light sign in the front window. It's still lit, as if the bar is still open. But there is no bar. And the front door is opened by a tired-looking woman with a toddler clinging to her knee.

"What do you want?" she says.

"Uh, I'm looking for my girlfriend."

"You one of Devon's friends?" She squints at me. Not unfriendly. More like she needs glasses. She's not as old as I first thought. Maybe in her late teens.

I don't know anyone named Devon, but I nod. If Devon threw the party, I need to talk to him.

She sighs. "You help trash my house last night?" She swings the door wide open, and I can see the mess inside.

It smells vile, like piss and booze and cigarettes and vomit.

"No way," I say. "I left early. I'm really sorry though."

She shrugs and picks up the toddler. "Not your fault, I guess. No girls here though. Just my lazy-ass brother."

"Can I talk to him?"

She steps aside and motions toward a door decorated with a Tupac poster. I bang on the door and a muffled voice says, "Eff off, Cara."

Cara steps up to the door and opens it. "Watch your mouth, Devon," she says. "You got a visitor. And it's time to clean up."

Devon groans and rolls over in his bed, turning his back to the door.

"Unca Devvy sleepy," the toddler says.

"Not anymore, sweetie," Cara replies. She hands me the kid and steps across the room to yank her brother out of bed. She's pretty strong—or else he's wasted. Either way, Devon stumbles past me as Cara drags him into a small messy kitchen. I'm still holding the toddler, who starts to cry. Cara says to Devon, "This guy's looking for his girlfriend. Tell him what you know and then get your shoes on—there's broken glass everywhere. Haley and I are going to her Water Babies class—and this place better be clean by the time we get back. Understood?"

Devon nods as his sister takes Haley from me and leaves the room. He slumps in the chair and puts his head on the table.

"I was here last night," I say. "With my girlfriend, Amy." No response. "She was the one dancing with Shawna."

Devon lifts his head off the table, looks at me with bloodshot eyes and grins. "That girl is hot."

"Which girl?"

"Yours. Amy."

Amy is hot, and there's no point fighting every guy who says so. I learned that early on. So all I say is, "Did you see who she left with?"

"Nah. I was busy. In my room, ya know."

"You know Shawna though, right?"

"Yeah."

"Got a number for her?"

Devon pulls out his cell phone and scrolls to the number. He holds the phone up to me, and I enter the number into my phone.

"Can I give you my number?" I ask. "In case you hear anything?"

Devon nods sleepily and hands me his phone. I enter my home and cell numbers and give the phone back.

"Thanks," I say as I step over a bong on my way to the door.

Chapter Three

Amy

My hands are shaking as I open the envelope and unfold the letter, which is printed on plain white paper. No fancy font, no signature. Black words on a white page.

Dear Amy,
    Don't be afraid. I don't want to hurt you. You don't know it, but you need me.

If you do as I ask, you will only be here a week. If not—well, I know you are a smart girl. In a week you will be free to go back to your life, if you still want to. There are clean clothes in the baskets. With any luck, you will be out of here before you need to do laundry. I hope the food is to your liking. The lights go on and off automatically. So does the heat and air conditioning.

Your task is this: Every day, write a short essay (one page, single-spaced) on one of the Seven Deadly Sins and the part it has played in your life. In case you have forgotten, the seven deadly sins are lust, greed, gluttony, sloth, envy, wrath and pride. Paper and pens are in a drawer in the kitchen. When you have finished each essay, please "mail" it through the slot in the door. The door is reinforced steel, so you will only hurt yourself if you try to break it down. The apartment is soundproofed;

screaming will not help you. Please take this assignment seriously, and do not submit more than one essay per day.

I look forward to reading your first essay.

Of course, there is no signature. I look up from the letter and stare at the door. I hadn't noticed the slot before. It's tiny, about the size of two cigarettes laid end to end. My heart is pounding and my mouth is dry. I cling to the words *I don't want to hurt you*, but the terror is coming—I can feel it in my bone marrow. And in my bowels. I throw the letter down on the table and lurch to the bathroom. There is no laxative like fear. My entire body is sweating, as if I have run a marathon. Then I start to shake, and I sit sobbing on the toilet. I am a prisoner. My prison is a white room with no windows.

And I have to write my way out. I hate writing.

When my guts stop cramping, I splash my face with cold water and dry it on a white hand towel. For some reason, seeing streaks of mascara on the towel makes me feel better. There is no mirror in the bathroom. I probably look like shit, but that's the least of my worries. There's a big magnet on our fridge at home that says, *Crying is all right in its own way while it lasts. But you have to stop sooner or later, and then you still have to decide what to do.* The guy who wrote the *Narnia* books said that. Not sure what he had to cry about. After my dad moved out, Mom cried for days, locked away in her room. Then one day she just stopped, and I haven't seen her cry since. A single tear trickles down my cheek, and I brush it away. I need to decide what to do. I won't stop being afraid until I'm out of here, but I'll have to live with that.

The phrase *I'm not going to hurt you* keeps running through my head. If it's true, then all I have to do is write seven stupid essays and I will be set free. If it's not true, then I need to protect myself and figure out a way out of my prison. It would help if my brain didn't feel like sludge. Dark and thick and slow-moving. I look around the main room for something to block the door. There is no heavy furniture other than the mattress on the bed. I grab a corner and drag it toward the door. It is very heavy. Or I am very weak. Or both. But at least if my kidnapper tries to come into the room to rape me or kill me, I'll know about it.

When I get the mattress in place, I kneel on it and try and peer through the slot, but I can't see anything. And it's way too small for me to get my hand through.

And what good would it do to wave my hand out a letter slot anyway? Even though the letter said not to, I scream into the slot. "Help! Help!" I feel ridiculous, but I keep screaming until I go hoarse. Then I pound on the door for a while, but nothing happens except that my hands start to bleed. I flop back onto the mattress and close my eyes.

When I wake up, the light in the room is different. Brighter. It feels like it might be lunchtime, so I make a cheese sandwich. The first few bites make me gag, but I force myself to swallow. If someone attacks me, I will need to have the strength to fight back. I wish I'd taken karate instead of dance. What good was a perfect split leap going to do me now? My dad used to watch this old TV show about a guy who could make a bomb out of a gum wrapper and a bungee cord and a single match. I wonder what he would do with bamboo cutlery, peanut butter and a wicker basket. I sure can't think of anything.

I need something metal. And sharp. I look around the room again. All the furniture is made of molded plastic. I stand up and hurl the night table against the wall, hoping it will shatter into sharp shards. It bounces. I smash the chair into the kitchen table, making a tiny dent.

I am suddenly very thirsty. When I open the fridge to get some juice, there it is, right in front of me—a white metal rack. I throw the little boxes of milk and juice on the floor and yank out the rack. I don't know how I'm going to get the metal rods out of the frame, but I have to try. My hands are still sore and swollen from pounding on the door, so I stomp on the rack until my feet hurt as much as my hands do. I wonder where my shoes are. And my phone. I wonder if anybody has missed me yet. I sit at the table and stare at the dent.

Gradually, the room darkens and the pot lights come on. The quiet is deafening. No street noise. No voices. No footsteps. Just the faint hum of what I figure is some kind of air-exchange system. I look up and see a small vent near the ceiling. No help there. I'll work on the fridge rack later. All I can do right now is write my first essay.

Chapter Four

Eric

It's been almost twenty-four hours since I last saw Amy. Ms. Lessard has called the cops, checked the hospitals and contacted Amy's dad. He says he hasn't seen Amy in weeks. I have been on the phone for hours. I call girls she dances with, girls she plays soccer with, girls who like to party. Guys she used to date, guys who want to get with her, guys on the swim team, guys on the chess team. It's a long list. No one has seen her. No one knows Shawna's last name or where she lives. Shawna isn't answering her phone. I leave message after message, text after text. *Call me. Call me. Call me.*

I fall asleep in the media room. Yes, that's what Mom and Dad call it. Not a TV room, a media room. Massive HD-TV, Bose surround sound, blackout shades, leather couches and chairs, fully stocked bar, commercial popcorn machine. My dad likes his toys. Not that he's ever around to enjoy them. Mom never comes down here—she prefers her office, on the top floor. And her white wine. And her tennis coach, Axel. Really. I bet his real name is Mike.

My phone wakes me up, and I grab it off the marble coffee table. I'm disappointed to see Ms. Lessard's cell number. Where the hell is Shawna?

"Have you heard from that girl? Shawna?" she says after we establish that neither of us has heard from Amy.

I sit up and try to focus. "No. I keep trying, but nothing yet. What do the police say? Are they looking for Amy?"

There's a pause before Ms. Lessard answers. It's like she's on a five-second delay. "They usually wait twenty-four hours to investigate a missing person, but since Amy's so young..." Her voice trails off. "They still think she's probably with a friend, but they're not taking any chances." Another pause before she says, "The police are on their way to see you, Eric. It's only a formality, a process of elimination. No one thinks you've done anything to her."

"They always suspect the boyfriend, right?" I say. I'd never hurt Amy. Ms. Lessard knows that. Doesn't she?

As if she's read my mind, she says, "I know you'd never hurt Amy, Eric. I told them that. They're just being, you know, thorough."

"Thorough," I repeat. The doorbell rings. I can hear my mom's heels clicking across the floor. "Gotta go, Ms. L," I say. "I think the cops are here. Thanks for the heads up." I end the call just as my mom's voice comes over the intercom.

"Eric. The police are here. Something about Amy. Please come up. We're in the kitchen."

When I get there, she is offering the two cops—one man, one woman— coffee. When they refuse, she pours herself a glass of white wine and says, "Should I stay?"

"Might be a good idea, ma'am," the man says, "since your son's a minor."

"How long will this take?" she says, looking at her watch.

"Not long, if Eric cooperates," the woman replies.

Mom laughs gaily, as if she's at a cocktail party, flirting with one of Dad's cronies. "Eric's very cooperative, aren't you, sweetie?" She perches on a stool by the counter and pats the stools on either side of her. "Make yourselves comfortable, officers. Eric, tell them what they want to know." She winks at the man, who blushes. Both officers stay standing.

"When did you last see Amy, son?" the man asks.

I hate it when men call me "son." My own parents never call me that. Why should anyone else?

"Last night," I tell him. "At a party on Washington Avenue."

"We heard there was a fight. Between you and Amy."

"Where'd you hear that?" I say.

"Doesn't matter. Is it true?"

"Yeah. But it was no big deal. She wanted to stay and dance. I didn't. Like I said, no big deal."

"What time was this?"

I think for a minute. We had gone to the party at around ten. Had a few drinks. Danced a bit. It was boring. I wanted to be alone with Amy. The music was way too loud, and everyone but me was on their way to getting wasted. Including Amy.

"I didn't check my watch. Probably around midnight."

The woman writes something in a notebook, and Mom takes a sip of her drink.

"Are you the jealous type, Eric?" the woman asks.

"Jealous? No. Not really."

"I hear your girlfriend was very attractive. And popular."

"Yeah. She was. Is." Why are they referring to her in the past tense? She isn't dead. I know she isn't.

"So that didn't bother you?"

"Not really. She was—is—friendly."

"Friendly." The woman turns the word over in her mouth like a hard candy.

"Yeah. As far as I know, popularity's not a crime."

Mom snorts, and the male cop raises his eyebrows at her.

"What did you do after you left the party, son?"

"I came home. Went to sleep."

"How did you get home?"

"I walked."

"From Washington Avenue? That's a long way."

I shrug. "I like walking."

"Anybody see you?"

"See me what?"

"Walking."

"I guess so. I mean, there were cars going by."

"And did you speak to your parents when you got in?"

"No. It was late. Dad's out of town. I didn't want to disturb Mom."

The cop turns toward Mom. "Did you hear Eric come in, ma'am?"

"Afraid not," Mom says. "I took a pill around midnight. Dead to the world until this morning. Sorry, sweetie," she says to me.

I shrug again. The officers exchange a glance that must mean the interview is over. The woman closes her notebook. The man puts a business card on the granite countertop. "Call anytime," he says. "If you hear anything. Either of you."

Mom nods and slides off the stool. She staggers a little and grabs the male cop's arm. "Oopsie daisy," she says.

I watch as she walks them to the door, weaving slightly. She waves goodbye and trills, "Toodles" as they get in their cruiser. Then she shuts the door and strides back to me. Her back is straight, her footsteps steady, her voice clipped and precise.

"What have you done this time, Eric?" she says.

Chapter Five

Amy

I'm not one of those girls who writes in her journal every day and dreams of being the next Stephenie Meyer or whatever. I never read anything unless I have to for school. Mom says that when I was little, I loved books, but somewhere along the way I stopped. She thinks it was because I got so serious about dance. I think it was because all the books we had to read for school were completely lame. I still get good marks in English though. So writing a few essays shouldn't be too hard. Especially if it will get me out of here. I push away the thought that it might not.

I get a pen and a pad of paper out of the drawer and sit down at the table. Which sin should I start with? I look at the letter again. Lust, greed, gluttony, sloth, envy, wrath, pride. The Seven Deadly Sins don't sound all that deadly. If I think about lust, I'm going to think about Eric. I wish we hadn't fought. I wish I'd left the party with him. I wish that chick Shawna had left me alone. No, I don't want to write about lust. Maybe sloth would be good. The image of a weird animal hanging upside down in a tree comes to my mind. That's not the kind of sloth I'm supposed to write about,

I'm pretty sure. I doodle on the pad for a minute—a daisy with two leaves—then start to write.

Sloth is another word for laziness. When I was little, Beth was always the one Mom called lazybones. Beth's not a morning person. I am. Mom says Beth and I are like our births. Beth took forever to come out. I tried to be born early. Beth moves slowly. I move fast. But Beth's not lazy. Not really. She just takes her time doing things. Like spreading peanut butter on her toast in the morning. Or getting dressed. It makes me crazy. But she's not lazy. Especially now, when she has to go to physio three times a week. And do exercises every day, probably for the rest of her life. She has to work so hard just to get from point A to point B.

No, the lazy one in my family is my dad. I remember him coming home from work and parking himself on the couch with a beer and a book. Even though she worked full-time too, Mom would still make dinner, do the laundry, help us with our homework, read us bedtime stories and make our lunches for the next day. Dad was supposed to take care of the yard and the house. You know. Mow the lawn. Clean the gutters. Let's just say that when they sold the house after the divorce, it was listed as a fixer-upper. Lazy. Slothful. That's my dad. Funny and smart, but not a ball of fire. Mom told me once that she fell in love with Dad because he was so laid-back and fell out of love with him for the same reason.

The real reason Mom fell out of love with dad is because his laziness almost got Beth killed. She was at a party one night and she called home for a ride, because the girl she went to the party with was too drunk to drive.

Mom and Dad had always said, Call for a ride. No questions asked. *Mom was asleep, and Dad answered the phone that night. He told Beth to call a cab, because he was too lazy to get off his ass and go get her. He told her he was "really into" the book he was reading. She got a ride with her drunk friend, who ran a red light and got herself killed. They had to use the jaws of life to get Beth out of the car. Her right leg was smashed. She had a concussion. Her pelvis was broken. All because Dad was too lazy to get out of bed. So, I guess you could say sloth kills. It doesn't sound like a deadly sin, but it can be.*

I've filled a page, and I don't have anything more to say about sloth. I do know which sin I'm going to tackle next. It's the one I'm feeling right now. Wrath. I'm so angry, I figure I can tear the fridge rack apart with my teeth. Not that I'm going to try. Mom would kill me if I wrecked my teeth after she spent so much to have them straightened. I try again to pull the rack apart, but all I manage to do is bend it a little. I slump over the table and rest my head on my arms. I'm so tired, but before I go to sleep, I need to find a weapon. And I need to "mail" my essay. I fold the paper in half and slide it through the slot in the door. I press my ear to the slot, but I can't hear anything, not even the sound of the paper falling to the floor on the other side.

I go into the bathroom to wash my face and pee. When I flush the toilet, I have a sudden memory of Dad telling me how to stop the toilet from running. Mom had been asking him to fix it for months. Jiggling the handle had stopped working.

"Take off the tank lid and lift up the rod and float for a few seconds. That should do it," he said. Thanks for being a lazy bum, Dad.

When I open the tank now, I find a metal rod attached to a float. If I take it apart, the toilet won't flush. If I don't take it apart, I won't have a weapon. I separate the rod and the float as carefully as possible—I want to be able to get it back together when I need to. The rod isn't long or sharp, but I feel stronger holding it. Less afraid. Before I go to bed, I take the pen and scrawl a big *DAY 1* on the wall across from the bed. Beside it I write the word *SLOTH*. Then I draw a tree with a sloth hanging from one of its branches. With the rod clutched in my hand, I crawl into bed. The pot lights dim and I sleep.

Chapter Six

Eric

My mom really should have been an actress, not a CEO. That whole flirty, "oopsie daisy" thing with the cops? Totally fake. She's not even tipsy, let alone drunk. And she's definitely not helpless. Or stupid. She just wanted the cops to think she was. She does that a lot. People (mostly men) underestimate her. They usually regret it.

This is a woman who started a dog-walking business when she was in high school and built it into a hugely successful company. There are DLD franchises all over North America. In case you were wondering, DLD stands for Donna Loves Dogs, the name she picked when she was sixteen. And yes, there's a heart in the logo. Mom hasn't touched a dog in years though. Won't have one in the house. She just sits up in her office and manages her empire. And plays tennis with Axel/Mike.

Now she's glaring at me as if I've made a mess on the carpet.

"Do I need to call Richard?" she asks.

Richard is Mr. Franks, the lawyer she keeps on retainer. I'll admit he's come in handy in the past. But she hasn't had to use his services—not for me anyway—in a long time. He read me the riot act when he got me off on the whole assault thing. Which was all a huge misunderstanding.

But I listened. And Amy has made it pretty clear she doesn't date losers or criminals. So I'm not that guy anymore. No matter what Mom thinks.

I shake my head. "I haven't done anything wrong, Mom. Really."

"So you have no idea where Amy is?"

"Nope."

"And you last saw her at a party? In a bad neighborhood?"

I nod. For the first time, I start to feel really afraid. For Amy. For myself. This isn't a game or a joke. This is real. Mom must see the fear in my face because she stops glaring and puts her arm around me.

"When was the last time you ate?" she asks.

I shrug. I honestly can't remember.

"Time for brinner then," she says. When I was little we used to have brinner—breakfast for dinner—all the time. Just her and me, sitting in front of the TV in our old house. Watching reruns of old shows like *Gilligan's Island* and *F Troop*. We haven't had brinner together in years. Not since her business took off and we moved.

I sit at the counter and watch her fry the bacon, scramble the eggs, put bread in the toaster. She looks over at me and smiles. "Just like the old days, huh," she says. She was always good at reading my mind.

I nod and say, "Have you called Dad?"

She shakes her head. "Should I?"

I shudder. The last thing I want is for Dad to take charge. That's what he does for a living. Hostile takeovers. He'd have Mr. Franks over here in a hot second. "No. Not unless I get arrested." I manage a weak laugh.

"Not funny," she says. "And those cops were idiots anyway."

"Even idiots can make an arrest."

"Not without evidence they can't," she says. She puts a plate of food in front of me and starts to eat scrambled eggs from the pan. "So what's your plan?"

"I've been trying to find this girl named Shawna. She was with Amy at the party. She isn't calling me back though."

"That's it?"

I take a bite of toast and watch her while I chew. She has a bit of scrambled egg on her chin, but otherwise she looks the way she usually does. In control. I'm sure if I asked her to hire a private detective, she would do it. I'm sure she wants to. But I want to find Amy myself. I want to be the one. Not some stranger.

"It's a start," I say. "And there's this guy named Devon. The party was at his house."

"Okay," she says. "How about—"

I cut her off. "Remember what Mr. Franks said last year? That I had to start taking responsibility for my actions?"

She nods.

"Well, let me do it then."

"But you just told me you're not responsible."

I get up, leaving most of my brinner untouched. "You know what I mean, Mom."

She turns away from me and runs some water over the frying pan. "I suppose I do," she says. "But this is serious, Eric. If the cops come back, I'm calling Mr. Franks. You are not to talk to them without both of us there. Do you understand?"

This is starting to feel like an episode of *Law & Order*. The kind where it turns out that the boyfriend chopped his girlfriend up and put her in the freezer. Except, I didn't.

Before I go to bed I try calling and texting Shawna again. No answer. No reply. Just before I fall asleep, my phone buzzes with a text from an unknown number.

Devon saw something.

I text back. *Who is this?*

Cara. Devon's sister. Come by tmrrw morning.

K. I reply.

The screen goes dark. My dreams are full of chainsaws, blood and bones.

Chapter Seven

Amy

In my dream, a skeleton dressed in a cheerleading costume is repeatedly poking me in my right breast with its bony finger. For some reason, this makes me laugh—at least, in my dream. Then I open my eyes and realize I am still in the white room. I am lying on the toilet rod. Being jabbed doesn't seem funny anymore. I'm going to have a bruise for sure. The only good thing is that no one tried to kill me while I was asleep. And I must be losing weight because my skirt feels loose. That's a bonus.

When I get up and go to the bathroom, it suddenly occurs to me that there might be hidden cameras. I wonder if someone is watching me pee. I put down the lid of the toilet and stand on it, peering into every corner. I don't see anything out of the ordinary, unless there's a camera in the showerhead. Just in case, I unscrew the showerhead and run water over it. I've already decided not to take any showers. I need to be able to hear what's going on at all times.

Then I check the main room. Slowly. Carefully. I consider the pot lights. The ceilings are, like, twelve feet high. And a camera in a pot light would just show the top of my head anyway.

And only when I was underneath it. The only thing that looks remotely like a camera is a peephole high up on the door. I stand on the recycling bin and look out. Or try to. Nothing. It must only work in reverse. I climb down, tear up some paper and wet it at the sink. When it's turned into mush, I climb up again and stuff it into the peephole.

Even that much exertion makes me feel weak, so I sit at the kitchen table and eat an apple. Every bite makes me gag. I have no idea what time it is. It's daytime. That's all I know. And I have to write another stupid essay. I look over at my wall drawing and smile. For some reason, it makes me feel good to have decorated my prison. I got in trouble when I drew on the living-room walls when I was about six. It wasn't scribbling, exactly. It was a mural depicting a magical kingdom where I was a princess and my family and friends were my loyal subjects and I had a pet unicorn. I thought it was an excellent addition to the room. I'd never seen Mom so mad. She had just painted the room a lovely sky blue. I think that's what got me started. The blank blue canvas.

Thinking about how mad Mom was that day reminds me that today's essay subject is wrath. I get the pen and paper and start to write.

Are wrath and anger the same thing? Wrath seems much more serious. Biblical, almost. Not that I believe in the kind of god who smites people with his wrath. Although it would be totally okay for him or her to smite whoever has put me in this room. I hope to have the chance to do some smiting myself. I used to have a really bad temper. When I was little, I was always having hissy fits about one thing or another. The temperature of the milk on my cereal (very cold). The arrangement of my stuffies on my bed (alphabetical, if you can believe it). I sat through a lot of time-outs. I still don't take criticism well. Never have. But I figured out in about grade seven that if I wanted to get away with stuff, I needed to stop freaking out all the time. I needed to be agreeable. So I stopped. And it worked. I got away with murder. And I was a lot happier. So was everyone else. And happier parents aren't nearly as alert. Trust me.

Once in a while I still get really angry. When it's the right thing to do. Like when I caught my old boyfriend, Gabe, kissing that slut Jasmine. I went off on them like a cherry bomb on the fourth of July. Haven't talked to either of them since. Not one word in three years. Silence is golden, right?

So when is wrath okay? I know Mom was right to be furious with Dad after Beth's accident. But her anger destroyed their marriage. Mostly because it wasn't hot anger. It was cold. She froze him out. Silently. And he couldn't take it anymore. And I was angry at him too. But Beth wasn't, and she was the one who got hurt. She forgave him long ago. But Mom and I still haven't. I'm supposed to visit him more than I do. But he's got a girlfriend now—Marlene something-or-other—and I can't stand her. When I see them, Dad gets mad at me for being rude. So it all comes full circle, doesn't it? But right now, staying mad is going to help me get out of here. I need all the help I can get.

I put the pen down, rip the page off the pad and fold it up. After I slip it through the slot in the door, I take the pen and write *DAY 2—WRATH* on the wall.

Next to it I draw a hand throwing a lightning bolt. The hand is hard to draw, but I do a pretty good job. Writing and art in one day. Mom would be so proud.

I think about going back to bed, but I'm worried that I'll lose all my muscle tone if I sleep too much. I have to eat. I have to stay fit. So I run laps around the apartment, which must look insane. When I'm too tired to run anymore, I lie down on the floor to stretch. From the floor, the ceiling looks miles away. I turn to look at my drawings and notice a pile of white dust on the carpet near the wall. I crawl over and stick my finger in it. It's gritty. Not cocaine then. Probably just as well. I need to stay focused. When I sweep my hand over the wall, my palm comes away white. I look up at the rows of glass block and suddenly I know what I need to do.

Chapter Eight

Eric

When I get to Cara's house the next morning, I wonder if it's too early to knock on the door. But then I remember the little girl. What was her name? Haley. Little kids don't sleep in, do they?

The door opens before I can knock. Cara is wearing yoga pants and a tight gray hoodie, and Haley is in a pink tutu.

At eight o'clock in the morning. No wonder Cara looks tired.

"I'm a bal-reena," Haley says.

"Nice tutu," I say.

Haley twirls away into the living room, where the TV is on. All traces of the party are gone. The house smells like lemons.

I follow Cara into the kitchen. There are red place mats on the old wooden table, and the counters are clean and uncluttered.

"Coffee?" Cara says, holding up a bright red mug. "I'm on my third cup." She laughs. "Only way to keep up with Haley."

"I'm good," I say. "Where's Devon?"

"At work, believe it or not. Valet parking at the Delta."

"Did he tell you what he saw?"

She takes a sip of coffee before she speaks. "He told me he saw Amy and Shawna leave the party together."

"And?"

"And he remembered the make and model of the car they got into. He's into cars. Always has been."

"So?"

Cara frowns at me. I must have sounded impatient, but I'm not sure how this information helps me. Especially if the car is something generic. Like a silver Honda Civic. Or a beige Camry.

"Did he get a license-plate number?" I ask.

"Nope, but the car was some deluxe hybrid thingie. I wrote it down when he told me. He doesn't know I called you. Doesn't want to get involved. The cops will question him sooner or later though. He'll be involved whether he likes it or not. So will I. So I figured the least I could do is give you a heads up." She digs a scrap of paper out of her pocket and hands it to me.

BMW ActiveHybrid 750 Li dark gray or black

I wonder how many BMW hybrids there are in the city. Maybe the information will keep the cops off my back though. I look up at Cara, who smiles and says, "Hope it helps. And don't worry about me and Devon. We can deal. Won't be the first time." For a minute she looks like any teenage girl. Blue nail polish, messy ponytail, smudged mascara, nice ass. I can't believe I'm looking at another girl's ass when Amy is missing. Then Haley bursts into the room, singing, "Fruit salad yummy yummy!" at the top of her lungs. Cara picks her up and dances around the room with her as I make my way to the door.

As I'm about to leave, Cara says. "Keep me posted, okay?" I nod, and Haley pats my face with a sticky little hand. "Bye-bye, Ewic," she says.

When I get to the police station, I can't remember the names of the cops who questioned me.

"I have information about the Amy Lessard case," I say.

The woman at the front desk, whose name tag says *Volunteer*, barely looks up from the game she's playing on her cell phone. "The what case?"

"Amy Lessard. The girl who went missing. I talked to two cops. A man and a woman."

"Well, that sure narrows it down," she says sarcastically. She turns her back on me and picks up the desk phone. After a brief conversation, she points to a bench in the waiting area. "Have a seat. Someone will be out to talk to you." She goes back to her game.

Half an hour later, I'm still waiting. I need to be out looking for Amy. I go back to the desk and ask for a piece of paper and a pen.

"What for?" the troll asks.

I resist saying that I want to stab her with the pen. "I have to go. I'll just leave a note."

She shoves a small pink message pad at me, along with a chewed-up Bic stick pen. I write Amy's name and the date at the top of the page, followed by *Last seen getting into a BMW ActiveHybrid 750 Li—black or dark gray*. I don't leave my name or phone number. When I hand the pad back to her, she tears the top sheet off and impales it on a spike on her desk. There are a lot of messages on the spike. Some of them are faded and curling. I guess volunteers don't take an oath to serve and protect.

I walk from the police station to the only BMW dealer in town. No one's going to believe I'm in the market for a BMW hybrid. But they might believe I'm an intern doing research for an article on green vehicles. So far, that's my plan.

When I stroll into the showroom, no one pays any attention to me. I find the 750 Li and walk slowly around it, crouching to inspect the tires. I mutter into my cell phone, as if I'm taking notes. After about ten minutes, a young guy in a dark suit approaches me.

I stick out my hand and introduce myself. "Carl Woodward. I'm researching an article about green cars. You know. Fuel efficiency, sustainability. I heard the BMW is very advanced."

He nods and says, "BMW hybrid technology is second to none."

"But aren't they kind of, uh, out of reach for most people?"

He laughs. "You might say that. But we still move lots of them."

"So, this model." I point to the 750 Li. "How many of these have you sold?"

"Let me check my files," he says. "Don't want you printing any misinformation."

"No, sir," I say, trailing him into his office.

He gestures to a chair, and I sit while he consults his laptop. "Here we go," he finally says. "Nationwide year to date—almost two hundred."

"And locally?"

"Locally, about twenty."

Twenty. My heart sinks. The salesman's eyes flick over to the showroom, where a man and woman are circling one of the sedans.

He stands up and hands me a brochure. "For the specs," he says.

"Anyone else I could contact? For a human-interest angle. A happy customer, maybe."

He shakes his head as he ushers me out. "No can do, Carl. Client confidentiality and all that."

Like he's a doctor or a lawyer. Or a priest.

I stand outside the dealership, pretending to talk on my phone. If he takes the couple for a test drive, maybe I can get back into his office and read his files. But the couple comes out on foot a few minutes later. Lookie-loos. Just my luck.

I start walking to the bus stop. My phone rings and I'm so startled, I almost drop it. Maybe Amy has turned up. But it's not Amy. It's her dad, Charlie, ready to play "Blame the Boyfriend."

Chapter Nine

Amy

Last summer my mom made me help her tile the kitchen backsplash. She said it would be fun. It wasn't. It was messy and boring. And it took two days. Two days I'll never get back. Mom said, "Someday you'll be glad you know how to do this." I couldn't imagine how that might be true. Until now. The white powder is dried grout.

Grout is what holds the glass blocks in place. Grout can be removed. It's hard work, but it can be done. You just need the right tools. All I have is a toilet rod. That will have to do.

First problem—how to reach the glass blocks. I have two plastic tables (one large, one small), one plastic chair, a mattress, three wicker baskets and a recycling bin. I shove the kitchen table against the wall and drag the mattress next to it. If I do fall, at least I won't break my neck. I empty the baskets. They are full of clothing: yoga pants, T-shirts, underwear. I kick the clothes into a corner. No way am I going to wear that shit, no matter how gross I get. I position the baskets upside down on the table. They are fairly sturdy, but not exactly solid. Enough to support my weight, I hope. I'm still nowhere near the glass blocks. The recycling

Deadly

box goes on next, then the small table
and finally the chair.

Second problem—I'm deathly
afraid of heights. Phobic, almost. I lie
down on the floor for a few minutes and
force myself to take long, slow breaths.
I am sweating again, and it's not just
from exertion. Fear twists my guts, and
I stumble to the bathroom and throw up
the apple I just ate. What if I starve to
death? What if I fall? What if I can't
reach the glass blocks? What if my
kidnapper comes in and finds me trying
to escape? What if…

"Pull yourself together, Amy," I say
out loud. That's what Mom always says
to me when I get upset. The sound of
my voice in the apartment is strange
but sort of comforting. Only one person
knows where I am, but my voice
reminds me that I still exist. Me. Amy
Lessard. Daughter. Sister. Girlfriend.

Soccer player. Dancer. I stick the toilet rod in the waistband of my skirt and talk to myself as I start to climb.

"You can do this, Amy. The table is solid. You are strong. You don't weigh much. The baskets will hold you. The recycling box is stable. You're okay. Take a deep breath. Keep going."

The tower is wobbly, to say the least. But I take it slowly. Very slowly. And I don't look down. I can't afford to be dizzy.

When I get to the chair, I kneel at first. I'm terrified, but I'm still not quite high enough to reach the grout. Slowly, very slowly, I stand up. "Ta-da!" I whisper when I'm upright. I feel like I'm in a really low-budget circus act. Amazing Amy and the Leaning Tower of Doom. The chair shifts, and I put one hand on the wall to steady myself. Vomit rises in my throat, but I swallow it down. I take the toilet rod out of my waistband and poke at the grout. A small trickle of powder slithers down the wall to the floor. I'm in business.

I have no idea how long I chip away at the grout. If I had to guess, I'd say a couple of hours. The light changes in the room, and my shoulder and neck start seizing up. My legs start to shake. The pot lights go on. I climb down before I fall down. The pile of grout dust on the floor has grown, but it's going to take a long time to loosen even one of the blocks. I need to eat and rest. Conserve my energy. Give my arm a chance to recover.

I splash water on my face at the kitchen sink and then make another cheese sandwich. As I eat, I wonder what's going on outside these four walls. Has Mom called the cops? Is Dad freaking out? Is Eric still mad at me for wanting to stay at the party? I put the sandwich down. The party. I was dancing with that girl, Shawna. I remember her getting us wine coolers. And I remember getting into a car with her. After that— nothing. I lie back on the mattress and close my eyes. My last thought before I sleep is, why would Shawna drug me?

When I wake up, I feel like crap. I smell bad, and my neck, shoulder and arm are on fire. A hot shower would help, but I can't do that. The tower looms over me, and I groan. I have to get up there again soon, but first I think I'll write my stupid daily essay. Get that out of the way. I sit with my back against the wall and write. It hurts even to hold the pen.

"Greed is good." That's what the Michael Douglas character says in that movie Wall Street. *I kind of agree with him. I know greed can get out of hand. Like when someone is greedy*

for power and kills people to get it. But if you're not a bit greedy, aren't you kind of passive? Dad used to call me Greedy-guts. I always wanted more— the last cookie, my sister's Barbie dolls, another push on the swings, extra butter on a bucket of popcorn at the movies. And I usually got what I wanted. My greed didn't hurt anybody except me. My sister was happy to share her toys. I was the one with cavities and a fat ass. So why is greed bad? Is it because you don't really need the things you're greedy for? Or you want something just so no one else can have it? Is it greedy to want money if you're poor? Is it greedy to want love if you're lonely? Is it greedy to want someone else's boyfriend? Last year I was going out with Jason Broderman. Nice guy. Hot. Not superbright. Eric was on-again, off-again dating this chick named Nicki. I thought Eric was cute and funny and smart. I decided I would be better for him than Nicki. When Eric and Nicki had a fight one night at a party, Eric and I hooked up. Nicki switched schools after that. So was I greedy? Sure, I hurt Nicki and Jason, but Eric and I are really happy. Does that make it right? I think I know the answer to that, but right now I don't care.

If I'm going to escape, I need to be greedy for freedom. Really greedy. So right now, yeah, greed is good.

Before I fall asleep again, I scrawl *DAY 3—GREED* on the wall and draw a pirate's treasure chest next to it.

Chapter Ten

Eric

I always thought Mr. Lessard liked me. Before Beth's accident, he was all easygoing, friendly. "Call me Charlie," he'd say, or, "Sit down and take a load off." He was always offering me food, asking about my games. He used to play football in high school too. Back in the day. I've hardly seen him since the divorce. Amy doesn't want to hang out with him, and she hates his new girlfriend. But now, as I listen to him accuse me of hurting his "little girl," I realize that he has no idea who I really am. That I would no more hurt Amy than he would. Unless I'm reading him all wrong too.

"I don't know where she is, Mr. Lessard," I say for the tenth time. "I don't know what I can say to make you believe me. I love her."

He snorts. "You don't know anything about love," he says.

"Maybe not," I say. My phone beeps—incoming call—and I tell Mr. Lessard I have to go. I don't care who is calling. It can't be worse than talking to good ol' Charlie. But it is.

"Eric, this is Detective Rayburn. We'd like you to come down to the police station. Some new information has come to light. We've got a few more questions for you."

"Like what?" Too late, I remember what Mom said about talking to the police.

"We'll talk when you get here."

"What if I don't come?"

"Well, Eric, we can't force you to help us. But it might be in your best interest."

"What do you mean?"

Detective Rayburn sighs. "You coming or not, son?"

"I'll get back to you," I say. Then I hang up and call my mother on her personal line. I think it's time to get Mr. Franks on board.

The room we meet in at the police station the next day is surprisingly nice. Cream carpet, dark wood conference table, comfortable chairs. There are six people in the room—and a video recorder. Mr. Franks, my mother and

I sit on one side of the table. Detective Rayburn and the two cops who came to my house sit across from us.

Rayburn reaches out to start the recorder, and Mr. Franks says, "Bit soon for that, don't you think, Mitch? My client isn't under arrest, is he?"

Rayburn shakes his head and lowers his hand. "Not yet," he says.

I have been instructed not to speak, but it's killing me. This is a total waste of time. I need to get out of here and find Shawna. Shawna is the link to Amy. Why don't they see that? While we're sitting here with our thumbs up our asses, someone may be hurting Amy. Or worse.

"A witness has come forward," Rayburn says.

"Ah," says Mr. Franks. "Do tell."

Next to me, my mother is the perfect picture of the ditzy, clueless mom, letting the big man do all the talking.

I can tell how pissed off she is by the way she clenches her fists in her lap.

"A young woman named Nicki"—Rayburn reads the file in front of him—"Nicki Morrison says she saw Eric and Amy together after the party. She says they were arguing, and Eric hit Amy." He looks down at the file again. "Apparently Eric has—shall we say—a history of violence."

I almost laugh. A history of violence. That was an awesome movie. I wonder if Rayburn has seen it. But there's nothing funny about his accusation. Nicki was my girlfriend back when the whole assault thing went down. We broke up when I met Amy. Nicki wasn't very happy. Neither was Jason, Amy's old boyfriend. But it's ancient history. At least, I thought it was until now.

"The charges were dropped," Mr. Franks says. "It was a boys' brawl that got out of hand. You know that as well as I do, Mitch."

"Ms. Morrison says Eric hit her when they were together." Rayburn picks up a photo and slides it across the table to us. Nicki with a black eye. A black eye she got when we were playing racquetball. She refused to wear goggles. Said she didn't need them. She was wrong.

"I—" I don't even get a second word out before Mr. Franks cuts me off.

"That all you got, Mitch?" he says. "Hardly evidence of a crime."

"There's more," Rayburn says. "Ms. Morrison has a friend named Shawna who says Eric drove away with Amy in an SUV that matches the description of his father's car. We're getting a warrant to search the car."

This time I do laugh out loud. Mom grips my arm, but I shake her off.

"You think this is funny, son?" Rayburn says.

"Hilarious," I say. "Come on, Mom. We're done."

We stand up and leave the room. Mr. Franks is close behind.

"I told you not to speak, Eric," he says. "I can't help you if you incriminate yourself."

We all speed-walk to the parking lot. Before Mom and I get in our car, I apologize to Mr. Franks.

"I'm sorry, but they are so full of shit."

"I'm listening," he says.

"Amy and Shawna got into a Beemer hybrid that night. I found a witness. A good one. My dad drives a Lexus, and it's not even a hybrid. Nicki's just a jealous bitch. And she's the link to Shawna."

"You're sure about this?" Mom asks.

"Positive. And I'm going to prove it."

Mr. Franks frowns at me. "I'd rather you let me handle it, Eric." He turns to my mother. "I can put Pete on it right away, Donna. Find this Shawna girl, find Amy."

Before my mother can speak, I say, "Twenty-four hours, Mr. F. That's all I ask. If I haven't found Amy by then, you can call in whoever you like."

"Donna?" Mr. Franks says.

Mom nods. "Twenty-four hours, Eric. Then it's out of your hands."

"For the record, I don't like it," Mr. Franks says.

Mom laughs. "You never like anything."

"I like keeping my clients out of jail," he says.

I salute him as he drives away.

We drive home in silence. Mom doesn't ask me what my plans are, and I don't tell her. She still hasn't suggested calling Dad. Maybe she thinks this is a good test of my character. If I fail… I can't fail. Amy is depending on me.

Chapter Eleven

Amy

I can't believe how much I'm sleeping. When I wake up, it's light again and I'm starving. I wish I could make toast, but there's no toaster. The first thing I'm going to eat when I get out of here is toast with organic peanut butter and banana. I fill a bowl with a mix of the disgusting cereals and pour some milk over it. It's not as bad as I thought it would be.

Sort of nutty. I have two bowls, and then I eat an orange. I sit at the table for a while, trying to get up enough energy to climb my leaning tower. I ache all over now, but I can't let that stop me. I know the police must be looking for me, but I can't count on them finding me.

There must have been a lot of bran in the cereal. I stagger to the bathroom and take the most explosive dump of my life. The smell is beyond gross. I remember when my dad tried to convince us to save water by posting that stupid rhyme in the bathroom—*If it's yellow let it mellow; if it's brown flush it down.* Who knew I'd ever agree with him. Now I hope I can remember how to put the toilet back together. I have a sudden longing for my dad. The dad before Beth's accident. The fun dad. The dad who always had time to watch me dance. The dad who made waffles on Sunday mornings. The dad who could fix anything and never did.

The toilet is pretty easy to put back together. Maybe I have a future as a plumber. Butt crack and all. I hike up my skirt, flush the toilet twice and then take the rod out again.

Before I climb the tower, I do the stretching routine we always do before dance class. It's sort of a fusion of yoga and Pilates, and it's meant to be done slowly. I try not to rush, but it's hard. I want to get back to work. I breathe deeply as I stretch, hoping it will calm me. Mom took up meditation after Dad left. She's always trying to get me to go. Now I wish I had.

When I feel a little more limber, I climb the tower again. It wobbles a bit, but I'm not as scared as I was yesterday. I'm totally focused on what I have to do. I chip away at the grout until my arm starts shaking uncontrollably. I take a lunch break, have a short nap and get back to work. The grout pile on the floor is growing.

As I work, I wonder again what's going on outside this room. Has my picture been on the front page of the paper? If it has, I hope Mom gave them the one of me that I use as my Facebook profile picture. Eric took it at the beach a while ago. I'm laughing and tanned and my hair looks great. Are the police interrogating Eric? Has anyone tracked down Shawna? Is Mom freaking out? Is Beth okay? Has someone started a *Help Find Amy* Facebook page? Maybe I'll be able to sell my story to, like, *People* magazine when I get out. Maybe I'll write a book. A bestseller. Mom would be so proud. And maybe I could buy her a nice house and a decent car. Take us all on a vacation. That's not greedy, is it? To want to be free and have a nice life?

On my next break, before I eat and nap again, I sit on the mattress and write about envy.

Right now, I'm envious of anyone who has their freedom. How can that be a sin? To want to feel the sunshine on my face? To hear Beth and Mom singing silly duets while they make dinner? To taste a strawberry-mango smoothie? To smell Mom's chocolate chip cookies? To see Eric's smile?

No, I think envy is a sin when you want something that someone else has and you want to take it away from them. And yeah, I've felt envy lots of times—even when I was really little. I remember when my friend Molly got Surf City Barbie for her birthday. I wanted it so much, I convinced myself it was okay to "borrow" it. It wasn't. Molly never forgave me. Seriously. For years she called me Barbie-stealer.

Now I'm mostly envious of people's cars or houses or clothes. But I don't do anything about it. And I don't think it hurts me to want a Beemer or a Prada bag. Maybe envy hurts you if it makes you hate your own life. Right now, my life—not my life in this room but my regular go-to-school, make-out-with-my boyfriend, go-to-a-dance-class life— seems pretty great. Better than great.

I wonder why we say someone is green with envy and we also call jealousy the green-eyed monster. Why green? Why not orange? Or puce, which is a gross color. Green is a great color. Think grass and emeralds and limes and Kermit the Frog and Granny Smith apples. When I get out, I'm going to be green with joy.

So is jealousy a form of envy? Isn't jealousy about being insecure? I wasn't jealous of Nicki when she was dating Eric. I was envious. I wanted him for myself. So I took him. I bet Nicki still calls me the boyfriend-stealer. But if I said I regretted what I did, I'd be lying (which must be some kind of sin). But I kind of miss Nicki sometimes. And Molly.

As I finish the essay and start to fold it up, I hear something outside the door. A scratching sound, followed by a sort of wheezing noise. Someone is there. I'm sure of it. I watch the door handle, waiting for it to turn, waiting for my captor to enter. My heart pounds as I clutch the metal rod in my hand and prepare to defend myself, but nothing happens. The sounds stops, and I crawl over and peer through the slot in the door. As usual, I can't see anything. Was it my imagination? Am I going crazy? I shudder and push my latest essay through the slot.

DAY 4—ENVY I write on the wall. Then I draw a horned monster with huge eyes and dripping fangs. Envy. And because I have no green pen, I scrawl an arrow pointing to the monster and add the word *green*. Then I get back to work on the grout. I'm no longer afraid to climb the tower. I scamper up it like I'm Jack and it's a beanstalk. My toilet rod is my magic wand. I work until my arm goes numb, and then I sleep again.

Chapter Twelve

Eric

The next day after school (Mom won't let me skip anymore), I borrow Mom's car and drive out to where Nicki lives. Amy calls Nicki's neighborhood "the suburb without a soul." Not very nice, but true. All the houses look the same. Nice enough, but boring. And getting a bit shabby. I haven't been here in over a year. The paint on Nicki's house is peeling, and the lawn is long and brown. Nicki's mom's old Hyundai is in the driveway. It needs a wash.

I ring the doorbell and brace myself. When the door opens, Nicki is standing there in a tiny denim skirt and a skimpy pink halter top. No bra.

"I knew you'd come," she says.

I follow her into the living room, where she curls up on the couch and pats the cushion next to her. I stay standing. The room is a mess. Greasy pizza boxes on the coffee table. Empty beer cans on the floor. Dust everywhere.

"Why are you telling lies to the police, Nicki?" I say.

Nicki pouts and says, "I don't know what you're talking about. I would never do that."

"I never hit you, and I never hit Amy. You know that."

"Do I?" Nicki shifts on the couch, just enough for me to see that she is going commando under her tiny skirt. I look away, but she knows I've noticed.

"Like what you see, Eric?" she says. "Now that Amy's gone—"

"What do you know about that? And where's Shawna? She a friend of yours?"

"Yeah, I know Shawna. Why?"

"She was the last person to see Amy, and she won't return my calls."

"Maybe I could help you with that."

I sit down in a stained La-Z-Boy recliner that smells like cat piss. "Maybe you should," I say. "I need to find Amy."

"She's probably with another guy, you know." Nicki twirls a strand of her hair between her fingers. Her nail polish is baby blue with glitter. "She's not exactly the faithful type. Not like me." She starts counting on her fingers. "Jamie, Gabe, that Swedish exchange student, that geek Fritz, Jeremy, Max, Jason. Oh yeah, and you. And those are only the ones since grade eight."

"Is that what this is all about? Me choosing Amy over you? You're nuts, you know that?" I turn to leave, and she leaps off the couch and runs to the door ahead of me. She tries to block me from leaving, but I shove her aside. She stumbles and falls on the tiles in the entryway.

"Those anger-management sessions didn't do much good, did they?" she says as she gets up. "Gonna be a bruise for sure." She runs her hand down her hip and smiles. "I'll be sure and document this." She grabs her phone from the hall table and snaps a picture of her bare thigh.

"Your word against mine," I say. "No witnesses."

"And who are the cops gonna believe? A big dumb football player with an old assault charge or a cute little cheerleader?" She strikes a coy pose, blue eyes wide, glossy lips parted. "If you know what's good for you, Eric, you'll forget about Amy."

"You're blackmailing me into being your boyfriend?"

"Whatever it takes," she says.

"You can't be serious," I say.

"Serious as herpes," she says. "Amy's not good for you. You'll see that soon."

I stand in the doorway and watch her prance into the kitchen.

"Want a beer?" She opens the fridge, and in the moment when her back is turned, I realize she has left her phone on the hall table. I slide it into the back pocket of my jeans and say, "I gotta go. Mom needs the car."

"You always were a mama's boy," Nicki says, taking a swig of beer.

"Yeah, that's me," I say as I leave.

"Good talk," Nicki says. "Call me, okay?"

I nod as I drive away. She waves and goes back into the house.

I am officially in crazy-town.

As soon as I get home, I check out Nicki's phone. The two people she's in constant contact with are Shawna the mystery girl and Jason Broderman, Amy's old boyfriend. I'm not surprised to see Shawna's name, but Jason's? That's just weird. I had no idea he and Nicki were friends. I scan the texts, hoping to get a clue to where Shawna lives. Or where she goes to school. No luck. Jason's texts read like they're from a really dumb six-year-old. A six-year-old obsessed with getting hammered and getting laid. I can't believe Amy ever went out with him. He can't even spell WTF.

I scroll through Nicki's photos. Nicki in a bikini. Nicki and her friends making that stupid duck face. Nicki and Shawna drinking vodka coolers and giving guys lap dances. Same old Nicki. I check her videos. More parties. More duck faces. Then I open a video of Jason screwing someone in a bathtub. The girl is Jeremy Bryson's little sister, Vanna, who looks like she might have passed out. She's only fourteen. Jason is groaning, "Amy, Amy, Amy" as he screws her. Rapes her, really. What I'm seeing makes me twice as scared for Amy. And I know I'll have to report the rape to the cops. Jason can't get away with that. I want to kill him—but I force myself to go back to the photos. I'm so freaked out, I almost miss the shot of Amy and Shawna kissing outside Devon and Cara's house. Next to them is a dark BMW hybrid SUV. I enlarge the picture. Amy's eyes are glazed over, and it looks as if Shawna is holding her up while they kiss. Jason is standing by the car, watching the girls, his hand down his pants. The next shot is of Jason and Shawna shoving Amy into the backseat. After that—nothing.

I put the phone down and go into the bathroom and puke. Then I lie on my bed and try to stop shaking. What I saw doesn't make sense to me. Jason, Nicki and Shawna drugged Amy and took her somewhere? But where? And why? And what was Jason doing to her? Would he rape her too? I can't get the sound of Jason saying Amy's name out of my head. But whatever he is doing, I have to stop him.

I go online to search for Jason's address, using the home number I found on Nicki's phone. I hit the jackpot right away. Broderman isn't exactly a common name. I use Google Street View to check out the address. He lives in a luxury condo development near the lake. I remember Amy saying something about how loaded his parents were. How they made a fortune tearing down nice old buildings and putting up big ugly ones. So the fancy condo makes sense. I need to get over there. I turn off Nicki's phone and stash it in my bottom drawer, under some old T-shirts. It's evidence of at least two crimes. I should take it to the cops right away, but I don't have time. I grab the car keys and am about to duck out the back door when I hear Mom say, "Oh good, you're back. I need the car."

Chapter Thirteen

Amy

I don't know what time it is when I wake up. A bit of gray light is coming through the glass blocks. I stare up at the place where I've been stabbing the grout, and I see something that makes me sit up and rub my eyes. The longer I look, the more certain I am. There's a sliver of brighter light between two of the glass blocks. Maybe it's moonlight. Maybe it's light from a streetlamp. It doesn't matter. I lie down and watch the stripe of light get brighter and brighter. The sun must be coming up. I eat an apple and a peanut butter sandwich, washed down with mango juice.

Then I take all the bras from the pile of fresh clothing and tie them into one long rope. I try not to think about the fact that whoever locked me up knows the kind of bra I wear and my size. At the end of the bra-rope I tie a pair of yoga pants. Then, just to be on the safe side, I sit down to write what I hope is my last essay. It's going to be a three-in-one. Pride, lust, gluttony.

Pride goeth before a fall. *My gramma, Dad's mom, used to say that to me. When I was little, I thought she meant a real fall—like off a ladder or something. It took me awhile to figure out that she wasn't talking about being proud of, say, scoring a goal in soccer. Or getting an A on a test. She was talking about being arrogant or boastful about it. And guess what? She was right. I found out the hard way in grade seven. I won a dance competition and got on TV. And I made sure everyone knew about it. And then all the girls I danced with stopped talking to me. And the girls at school called me a stuck-up bitch and a whore, among other things. They said I was sleeping with my lesbian dance teacher. In grade seven! To be honest, falling off a ladder would have hurt less. Anyway, I learned to shut up about stuff I do well. But it's weird—I still have a rep for being a bitch and a slut, even though I don't go around bragging anymore.*

And Eric still has a rep for being violent. I wonder how long that will last.

Speaking of Eric, I might as well get lust out of the way. Was it lust that made me want him? Maybe. Jason was so lame. Always crying afterward. And moaning my name. And telling me how much he loved me and how he'd do anything for me. Except figure out how to last more than three minutes. Standing next to Eric made the hairs stand up on my arms. Still does. That's all I have to say, other than I'm not on board with lust being a sin.

And gluttony? Well, it's disgusting, for sure. I mean, look at how many obese people there are. But a sin? There a lot worse things than stuffing yourself with Big Macs or KFC. Like hurting an animal or killing a child. Or just not caring about anything. What's that called? Apathy. That's a bad one.

So here's my updated list of the Seven Deadly Sins:

1. *Murder/violence*
2. *Hurting animals or children*
3. *Wrecking the environment*
4. *Greed*
5. *War*
6. *Gossip/trash-talking*
7. *Apathy about any of the above*

Notice that only one—greed—was on the original list. That's because being greedy for wealth and power can lead to all the other things on my list.

I put the pen down and flex my fingers. Still sore. So are my shoulders, my back, my legs. I fold the paper up and "mail" it through the slot. I write *DAY 5* on the wall. Next to it I draw a fat dude with an erection, falling off a ladder. Three sins in one. It makes me laugh. Writing on walls is awesome. It's like being three again. When I get out of here, I'm going to paint one of the walls in my room with that chalk-board paint. Then I can write on the walls all the time.

I tuck the Sharpie into my bra and tie my bra-rope around my waist before I climb the tower for what I hope is the last time. When I get close to the glass blocks, I feel something I haven't felt in days—fresh air on my face. It feels amazing, and it smells slightly like…water. And beer. The lake. I'm near the brewery at the end of the lake. I attack the grout like a maniac. Sweat pours down my face and back. My arm feels like it's going to fall off, but I keep going. The grout is coming away quickly now. Two sides of the block are free, then the third. I pull the Sharpie out of my bra. I hope it will write on glass. It does. I write in block letters *LOOK UP* and then my name, *AMY LESSARD*.

Then I get to work on the fourth side of the block. When I can see sunlight all the way around the block, I start to shove it out. I scream and swear at it as if it is my captor. "Bastard! Asshole! Jerk-off!" At last it starts to move. Slowly. Really slowly. When I get it to the edge, I stop pushing and tie my bra-rope to my toilet rod. I'm ready. Or as ready as I can be. I give one last shove to the glass block and it falls away, leaving me a small window. Way too small to climb out of, but not too small to get my hand and arm out. I inch closer to the window and shove the toilet rod out. The rope dangles from it and just before I start to scream, I hear the most beautiful sound in the world—the glass block hitting something and, a second later, a car alarm going off. I wave my bra-flag and scream, "Up here! Up here! Up here! Amy Lessard! Up here!"

I scream until the car alarm stops. And then I scream some more. I wave my bra-flag. I cry. And then I hear a new sound. Footsteps, followed by someone banging on the door and calling my name. There's a scuffle, and suddenly the door bursts open. I sink to my knees on the mattress, sobbing. It's over.

Chapter Fourteen

Eric

Once we're inside the room, I tackle Jason from behind and wrestle him to the floor. Amy is huddled on a mattress, crying, but as soon as Jason is down, she jumps up and starts to kick him. She is barefoot, and it must hurt every time her foot connects. But rage makes her ignore the pain.

"You bastard," she screams. "Did you do this to me?" She looks over at me, as if seeing me for the first time. Her cheeks are streaked with tears. "Did he?"

I nod.

He tries to roll away from her, but I've got his arms behind his back. One of her kicks connects with his balls. He shrieks and curls into a ball. Amy kicks him in the face.

"I need to tie him up," I say, struggling to hold on to him. He's a big guy—bigger than me, but not stronger. "Then I'll call the cops."

Amy stops kicking him and runs over to a weird pile of furniture next to the wall. She grabs something and tosses it to me. "I don't need this anymore," she says. Her voice is hoarse. She collapses on the mattress again while I tie Jason up with what appear to be bras. I don't ask. This is so messed up. I just want to get her out.

Once I have Jason hog-tied, I pick up his keys from where they've fallen on the floor. "Let's go," I say to Amy. "I can call the cops from outside."

"Not before he tells me why," she says. She gets up and crouches next to Jason. "Why, asshole? Why did you do this?"

"I love you, Amy," Jason whimpers. "I just wanted you to love me again."

"So you thought you'd kidnap me?"

"I thought if you had some time to yourself, away from him"—he jerks his head toward me—"you'd remember how good we were together, how much you loved me."

"I never loved you, Jason." Amy leans closer to him and spits in his face. "I barely even liked you."

"I wasn't going to hurt you, Amy. I was always going to let you go."

Amy rocks back on her heels and stares at him. "You're insane, you know that? Why the essays? The seven deadly sins." I have no idea what she's talking about. I can't even remember what the seven deadly sins are. I want to leave. Get her away from here. From him.

Jason squirms and mutters, "I saw it in a movie. I thought it was cool. And scary."

"You thought it was cool. And scary," Amy repeats, shaking her head. Her hair, which is usually shiny and thick, is lank and matted.

"Yeah," Jason says. "I'm sorry. Nicki said it would work. She said she'd get Eric back, and you'd be with me again."

"Nicki?" Amy sounds dazed.

"So Nicki's the criminal mastermind?" I ask.

Jason nods. "It was all her idea."

"Even the rape?"

Amy gasps. "What rape?" Her face is ashen, her eyes wide. She gets up and backs away from Jason, tripping on the mattress.

"Vanna Bryson," I say. "Jeremy's little sister. Jason raped her. Nicki took pictures. It's all on her phone. Which I have."

Jason groans. "It wasn't rape, man."

"Looked like rape to me," I say. "Statutory. Guess the cops can figure that out." I pick Amy up off the mattress, where she has curled herself into a ball. She smells bad, but I don't care. I look around the room before we leave. There is writing all over one wall. And pictures. Crazy pictures. An animal, a devil, a treasure chest, a lightning bolt and a fat man with a huge hard-on. The tower of furniture leads to a small opening in a row of glass blocks. I can see a little square of blue sky. I carry her out of the room, locking the door behind me.

She buries her face in my shoulder as the elevator drifts silently down to the ground floor. Once we're outside, I put her down on a low stone wall and drape my jacket around her shoulders.

"What is this place?" she says. Her teeth are starting to chatter.

"Some building Jason's parents own," I say as I call the police and ask for Detective Rayburn. "It's unoccupied. I guess that's why no one saw Jason bringing you here."

"How did you find me?"

"I followed him. He wasn't exactly hiding. Just being Jason. You know—stupid."

"But how did you know it was him?"

"Nicki took pictures of you and Shawna outside the party. And of Shawna and Jason putting you in the Beemer. You were pretty out of it. My guess would be Shawna put something in your drink."

"I don't remember anything past getting in the car," Amy says. "Nothing at all."

"I would have been here sooner, but Mom needed the car." The minute I say it, I realize how lame it sounds. "I mean, I had to have a car to follow him. But it looks like you figured a way out anyway."

Amy is silent.

Detective Rayburn finally comes on the line, and I say, "I found her. I found Amy. We're over by the lake. Near the brewery." I give him the address.

"We've been getting calls about some girl screaming and waving a flag near there," he says. "And some guy's windshield got smashed by a falling glass block. Squad cars are on the way. Anything to do with you?"

"Probably," I say. I turn to Amy, who is staring out over the lake. "You know anything about a glass block and a flag?"

She nods but doesn't speak.

"Yeah, that was Amy," I say. "I guess she had a plan."

"Smart girl," Rayburn says. "If you hadn't turned up, we would have been there soon though."

After I hang up, I sit beside Amy on the wall and put my arms around her.

"The cops will be here soon. They'll have a lot of questions. You want to call your mom first?" I punch in the number.

She nods and says, "Speaker" through clenched teeth. She is shivering uncontrollably now. I can hear sirens. Lots of sirens.

Her mom answers the phone. "Hello? Eric, is that you?"

"It's me, Mom," Amy says. Her voice is steady, even as her body shakes. "It's me, Amy."

Chapter Fifteen

Amy

Jason's trial won't happen for ages. He's locked up somewhere. Nicki helped the cops nail Jason, so they only charged her with aiding and abetting or whatever. She's free to run around blabbing about what a bitch I am. It's total bullshit. She may not have raped anyone, but she helped plan the whole thing. She paid Shawna. Nicki says it was all meant to be a joke. Jason was going to let me out after a few days. He wasn't ever going to hurt me. Tell that to Vanna Bryson. She charged him with rape. I charged him with kidnapping and unlawful confinement. We'll both have to testify. It will be worse for her. I got away. She didn't. Except for that first day, I never felt totally helpless. She must have, because she was. I hope she's okay, but I can't imagine that she is. My lawyer says I'm not supposed to talk to her. I'm not sure why. But I texted her anyway, to say I was sorry. She never texted me back.

I'm okay—barely. I see a therapist once a week. I have nightmares. I can't stand to be in any room with the door shut. Dr. Milne says that's normal, but it makes using the bathroom hell. My appetite is all over the place. I crave weird things that I haven't eaten since I was little. KD with hot dogs. Coke floats.

Mom gets me whatever I want. Beth sits with me and watches *Sex and the City* (which she hates). Eric comes over every day after school and stays until I fall asleep. Or longer. A couple of times I've woken up in the night, and he's been asleep on the floor beside my bed. No one says anything about him staying over. Dad calls every day. But none of them really understand. How could they? I know they're trying, but it's pretty lonely sometimes. Dr. Milne says it will get better. Mom says to trust Dr. Milne. I try.

My essays were all found in the glove compartment of Jason's Mom's SUV. His IQ really is smaller than his shoe size. The originals are all in an evidence locker somewhere, but I asked Detective Rayburn for copies. I showed them to Mom, and she couldn't stop crying and saying how proud she was of me. She even told me I had a gift. Maybe she's right.

One of the cops took pictures of my wall art. I have copies of those too. As well as photos of the Leaning Tower of Doom. I lay all the evidence out on my bed and look at it every day. I read the essays and let my feelings surge through me. Like an electric current. I'm furious at Jason, but I'm also furious at myself for ever dating him. I'm too lazy to make my bed, but I sleep so much it doesn't matter. I'm greedy for open spaces and the sound of laughter. I'm envious of my happy friends, who only want to talk about clothes and boys. I'm hungry for junk food, even though I'm starting to get zits. I'm not quite ready to have sex with Eric. But mostly, I'm really proud of myself. Proud that I used everything that was in me to escape. My brain. My muscles. My rage. My greed. I'm proud that I survived. And that's no sin.

Acknowledgments

Thank you, as always, to Andrew Wooldridge and the rest of the pod at Orca.

Sarah N. Harvey is the author of ten books for children and young adults. Some of her books have been translated into Korean, German and Slovenian, none of which she speaks or reads (although she is trying to learn Italian). Her novel *The Lit Report* has been optioned for a feature film. She will not be in it. Sarah lives and writes in Victoria, British Columbia. For more information, visit www.sarahnharvey.com.

Titles in the Series

orca soundings